THE BASICS OF HOSPITAL CHAPLAINCY

A basic introduction and fundamental guide to hospital chaplaincy

Ronald Mack, Sr.

D1292998

PRESS

Special thanks, respect, and God bless to Jeffrey Funk for making this publication possible.

TABLE OF CONTENTS

PREFACE

Fascinating flower gardens come in many forms and fashions. They present many colors of flowers bearing different fragrances and designs to reflect the majestic beauty and structure of God's creation. The hospital chaplain ministry is like a flower garden: it reflects the call, love and care one has for God's creatures of distinction.

As a hospital chaplain, you must approach your ministry as if working in a garden of majestic beauty structured by God's hands. You will be ministering to people of different races, sexual orientation, religion, economic background, social class, age, etc. You need to approach patients without prejudices. As a pastoral care-giver, you are obligated not to do anything that would hurt, upset or discount a patient's floral beauty.

The hospital chaplain must come into the presence of all patients as a channel of God's love and comfort, as one who brings comfort to the distressed, as one who is patient-directed and interested particularly in the patient's personal needs at the moment.

I spent years pursuing my call to hospital chaplaincy. I experienced what I call extreme difficulties in acquiring required training and connections to necessary resources in order to exercise my calling. I acknowledged God in my situation and He directed my path. It is that memory that prompts the writing of this book.

Like any explanation of God's handiwork, this one may not satisfy the expectations of some. Yet I am grateful to God for His call, my experiences and the clinical pastoral training I received from the Hospital Chaplains' Ministry of America (HCMA). I am thankful for the extent He enabled me to realize the value of hospital chaplaincy. I am grateful for the strength He has given me to pursue my call and complete this book.

There are some people I would like to acknowledge who were fundamental to my personal and professional development and without whom this book would not have been possible. I am greatly indebted to the vital influence of my seminary professors who stimulated my mind. I sincerely appreciate the exemplary mentoring by my HCMA Teaching Chaplain Jerry Wylie who helped guide me in understanding pastoral care in the healthcare setting. I am also thankful for the editorial advice given by the HCMA Executive Director Jeffrey Funk who helped clean up some of my grammar. I am also indebted to Doctors Community Hospital in Lanham, MD, where I received my clinical experience.

INTRODUCTION

The modern day hospital chaplain is provided many opportunities for engaging in a wide range of ministry activities in the different hospital environments. As a hospital chaplain, you will be called upon to minister to all types of people – of different ages, races, genders, religions, beliefs, nationalities, and social status – who are troubled by many problems. Some of their problems are severe life and death issues and some are not so grave. Nevertheless, the hospital chaplain's responsibilities are often to minister to a large group of people who come from various backgrounds and who are dealing with emotionally and spiritually disturbing difficulties of many descriptions.

A hospital chaplain is not a medical professional, psychiatrist, psychologist, or social worker. He or she is a clergy person who has received extensive and intensive clinical pastoral training and has met certain competency standards in order to be certified as a professional hospital chaplain. Because of this highly skilled pastoral care background, the hospital chaplain is able to assess people's spiritual and emotional distress so that he/she can minister effectively to them or make appropriate referrals. The hospital chaplain, in many cases, is a valuable link between patients and their physicians.

A hospital chaplain is a very important part of the healthcare team and offers spiritual counseling and emotional support to the sick, recovering, and dying patient. If the patient does not have his or her own minister, the chaplain often serves as a trusted friend and pastoral figure. The chaplain is often available to the emergency room, intensive care unit, and hospital staff to help with the distressed family or a critically ill or dying patient.

Entrance training (which involves 1600 hours of clinical pastoral education) and continuing education are a must and play a very important part and major role in the hospital chaplain's life and growth. I started my clinical pastoral training in July of 1999 with HCMA, after over 23 years as a pastor and evangelist. I completed my required training and received my certification as a Professional Certified Chaplain (PCC) with HCMA on May 23, 2001. There is a great need for others to recognize and accept hospital chaplaincy as a skilled and professional discipline and vital part of the healthcare community.

In addition to my clinical pastoral education with HCMA, I also trained with the Master's Divinity School of Chaplaincy. This chaplaincy program is recognized by the United States Chaplain's Association (USCA). This training provides certification levels for those whom God has called to the chaplain ministry. It equips the chaplain to provide pastoral care, biblical counseling, pastoral care giving to the sick, the terminally ill and their families. Program completion qualifies a person for USCA membership.

I want to make two things clear. First, ministering as a hospital chaplain is different from ministering as a pastor or evangelist. Just because you are well trained and experienced as a pastor or evangelist does not necessarily mean you will be an effective hospital chaplain. Second, I acknowledge my indebtedness to people who have been instrumental in my development as a chaplain. My HCMA Teaching Chaplain, Jerry Wylie, was very helpful to me. This would also include the Master's Divinity School Instructors: John Pugh, Ph.D., Walden University, William H. Ammon, Ph.D., Trinity Theological Seminary, Howard A. Eyrich, D.Min., Western Bible Seminary, Russell Vance, Ph.D., Trinity Theological Seminary, Ed Hinson, Ph.D., and Professor Ed Martin. These individuals are the source of my learning experience and contributors of the majority of materials included in this book. Some of the material is essentially as it was given to me. Other information has been retained but reinterpreted. A small portion is original with me.

This material is written and presented as an elementary guide for those who have little education and experience in hospital chaplaincy. Its purpose is threefold: First, it was written to help the reader examine the basic requirements for being a hospital chaplain. Second, this material is presented to help show the basic role of the hospital chaplain. Finally, this information is given to help encourage recognition and acceptance of the value of hospital chaplaincy in the healthcare setting.

It is my prayer that as you read this book, you will gain a deeper understanding and richer appreciation for the hospital chaplaincy. And I hope that some of you will be challenged to consider hospital chaplaincy as a ministry for yourself. If you do feel that God may be calling you into this dynamic and challenging ministry to the sick and suffering, please look at the HCMA web site: http://www.hcmachaplains.org, or call them at (714) 572-3626.

CHAPTER 1

Hospital Chaplains Work Environment

⎯⎯═ঃ৶●ぐ⊏⎯⎯

Most, if not all, hospitals work very hard to be a visible and important part of a community. Thus many of us probably have had some experience with a hospital. Many of you have certainly visited a hospital to see someone who was a patient there. Some of you have been there as a patient. But you may have never really had the opportunity to work in a hospital as a staff chaplain. In order to be an effective chaplain, you must become familiar with the hospital environment. There is more to being a chaplain than simply showing up at the hospital and making your presence known. As a hospital chaplain, you must be conscious of the environment in which you are called to minister. I encourage anyone who is contemplating entering the hospital chaplains ministry to arrange with the Director of the Pastoral Care Department so that you can make a special visit to the hospital for the sole purpose of observing first hand the environment you would be seeking to work in.

A hospital is a place where sick or injured people are given medical attention or surgical care. Although many hospitals today are involved in educational and research operations, a hospital can also be considered a dangerous place. It is a place where all types of diseases (some contagious) are present and where potentially harmful drugs and chemicals are used and stored. It is a place where hazardous materials are used and stored. You must have this aware-ness while ministering in the hospital.

There are different types of hospitals. For example, there are hospitals for children only (pediatric facilities), hospitals for seniors only (geriatric centers), hospitals for the mentally challenged (psychiatric institutions), and hospitals for specialized treatment (like a rehabilitation facility). I serve as chaplain in the acute care section of a multi-type hospital. It also has a nursing home facility.

If you were to take a training tour of an acute care hospital, you would first notice the cleanliness of the facility and busy activity of the workers. Hospital workers can be divided into two groups: medical workers (such as doctors, nurses, laboratory technicians, and physical therapists) and non-medical personnel (such as cooks, housekeepers, dieticians, maintenance workers, security, social workers, and chaplains).

The hospital chaplain functions as a very important part of the healthcare team. He/she must not only be able to intermingle with the other professionals but to interrelate and interact with them. Hospital chaplaincy is a specialized ministry with many demands.

My experience as a hospital chaplain allows me to share with you some of the different areas or departments in an acute care hospital. The emergency room (ER) is considered sort of a separate unit of the hospital. It is set up to handle situations relative to urgent medical conditions, injuries or accidents that must be treated imme-diately. You do not need a doctor's referral to go to an ER. The ER has a doctor in attendance 24-hours a day and is staffed by nurses who are specially trained in emergency care. When you enter an emergency room, you will see the admitting area and waiting room for patients and their families. Once admitted, the patient is taken to an examining room for examination. There is also a trauma room where severe cases are handled. Observation beds are used for patients who need to stay in the ER for a while.

The Intensive Care Unit (ICU) and Coronary Care Unit (CCU) are areas where very sick patients are placed. All these rooms are specially equipped with computerized monitoring systems. In addi-tion, built-in alarm systems warn the staff of changes in a patient's condition. The nurse's station is often located in the center of the unit so they can see into each patient's room.

The surgery department is where operations are performed. There are operating rooms (OR), scrub sink rooms for the surgeons and nurses, and sterilizing rooms for preparing surgical supplies. Once surgery is completed, the patient is moved to a recovery room (RR). In the RR the patient is observed closely until the effects of the anesthetics wear off. When it is determined that the patient is awake and alert, he/she is taken back to a regular room in the patient room (PR) area. Hospitals have different size patient rooms. Private rooms have only one bed. Semi-private rooms have two beds. Wards are rooms with three, four, or more beds. Keep in mind that as a hospital chaplain you may be called to minister to the patient or patient's family at any given moment, in any of these areas or departments.

The hospital chaplain must be familiar with emergency conditions and basic staff response as outlined in hospital policies and procedures. The chaplain must pay close attention to overhead announcements and follow the instructions of his/her supervisor. The chaplain must know the emergency codes in the hospital. Hospital Codes are subject to modification. For now, where I serve, a Code Red is notification of fire, smoke, or the smell of something burning. A chaplain must know the proper response. In the case of Code Red, the chaplain must rescue those in immediate danger, if safe to do so, and activate the fire alarm.

A Code Blue usually means someone is in cardiac arrest. The chaplain must go to the scene and be of assistance to the staff with the family or in any other way needed.

In my hospital, a Code Green is notification of a bomb threat. In such a situation, the chaplain must notify the switchboard operator and listen to any further overhead announcements.

A Code Yellow is notification of an internal or external hazardous material disaster. The chaplain must listen to overhead announcements and assist in sealing off the area and assisting victims, if needed.

A Code D is notification of an external disaster. The chaplain must listen to overhead announcements and report to his/her department.

An internal disaster is designated as a Code I in my hospital. The chaplain must listen to overhead announcements and report to his/her department.

A Code Pink is notification of child abduction. The chaplain must be alert and report any suspicious person or activity to security.

The chaplain must be familiar with the hospital administration and chain of command. As a chaplain, you must know what department you are part of and to whom you are accountable. The person responsible for total management of the hospital is the administrator. At my facility I am part of Volunteer Services/Pastoral Care Department and am accountable to the Volunteer Services Coordinator. At other facilities the chaplain may be under another department (like social services) or the Pastoral Care Department may be a separate department. For personal growth and development, the chaplain must also be accountable to fellow chaplains. This accountability can be realized through membership in chaplain organizations, such as United States Chaplain's Association and Hospital Chaplains' Ministry of America.

Many chaplains are employees of the hospital and receive a salary and benefits for the valuable service they provide to the patients, family members and medical staff. Other chaplains are Independent Contractors and receive a moderate stipend from the hospital for the professional services they provide. Some chaplains volunteer their professional services and receive no stipend or benefits from the hospital where they serve.

Two more important things, the chaplain must be familiar with posted signs and medical abbreviations. These signs and abbreviations are often found posted on the door of the patient's room. You may see signs such as, restricted visits, no visitors, etc. You might see medical abbreviations such as "NPO," which means nothing by mouth (and this includes serving communion to the patient). Below is a list of abbreviations that I have frequently observed in my hospital ministry.

a	Before
BM	Bowel Movement
BP	Blood Pressure

CCU	Coronary Care Unit
CHF	Congestive Heart Failure
EKG	Electrocardiogram
ER	Emergency Room
HBP	High Blood Pressure
HD	Heart Disease
HIV	Human Immunodeficiency Virus
ICU	Intensive Care Unit
IV	Intravenous
JCAHO	Joint Commission on Accreditation of Health Organizations
LPN	Licensed Practical Nurse
MD	Medical Doctor
NPO	Nothing by Mouth
OR	Operating Room
Phy Ex	Physical Exam
po	Post Operative
pt	Patient
RR	Recovery Room
RN	Registered Nurse
Rx	Prescription
SOB	Shortness of Breath
T	Temperature
TPR	Temperature, pulse and respiration
URI	Upper Respiratory Infection
UTI	Urinary Tract Infection
VD	Venereal Disease

There are some things about the hospital environment we can't know and will never know. However, basic knowledge of the hospital environment is and always will be a critical part of a hospital chaplain's training.

CHAPTER 2

Practical Aspects of Hospital Chaplaincy

———————

It is clear that hospital chaplains must have a love for others and have an impulse in their hearts to go to the hospital and share that love. That means they love to visit hospital patients. Hospital visitation is a chaplain on an encounter of love and divine direction with the intent of bringing hope, compassion and friendship to another. It is an act of Christian love. It means being present and active in the life of another.

I find hospital visitation to be very challenging. Professional boundaries are always a necessity, even to the hospital chaplain. The hospital chaplain must avoid the risk of upsetting, hurting, or making a patient uncomfortable by pushing any kind of personal agenda. There are many agendas a chaplain can push relative to his/her religious connection, ability to cope, prejudices, and personal and patient needs. Agendas can be classified as assumption, self-serving, hidden, escape, religious, prayer and Scripture, evangelism, and education.

Assumption Agendas

The need of the patient must not be based upon the chaplain's *assumption*. As a hospital chaplain, you must not assume that you know what the patient needs. You must not even assume that the patient needs or wants your pastoral help. You must not jump to conclusions. You need to allow the direction of the visit to be determined by the patient. It's very important to be open to the patient's lead. For example, in my hospital the Catholic clergy is very efficient in visiting their Catholic patients. However, I can recall many times, while visiting non-Catholic patients in rooms with a Catholic patient, where the Catholic patients requested that I minister to them also.

Self-Serving Agendas

Some people have a basic need to help others in order to gain acceptance and/or feel better about themselves. Outwardly they may appear very loving and self-sacrificing. In reality, they may be seeking to meet their own needs. In such cases a patient is viewed as a need to be met instead of a person who has value and is worth getting to know and understand. The *self-serving* agenda can be very harmful to a hospital chaplain (as well as the patient). Early burn out is a very strong possibility for the chaplain. Pushing self-serving agendas does more harm than good.

Hidden Agendas

Because of attitudes and actions stemming from feelings held deep inside, feelings the hospital chaplain may be blind to, he/she may unknowingly push a *hidden* agenda. Chaplains, like other human beings, have hidden feelings that can be excited when they encounter people of different race, sexual orientation, religion, economic background, social class, age, etc. As a chaplain, you must feel compelled to be open-minded about yourself and others and to regularly exercise the discipline of self-evaluation.

Escape Agendas

Even a hospital chaplain may find it difficult to cope in certain situations that make him/her very uncomfortable and uneasy. There are certain situations that may cause you to enter into an *escape* mode. It might be a smelly room, a jaundiced patient, sexual attraction, or a crisis involving a small child. It's important for you to understand what's happening when you feel an urgency to get away from certain situations.

Religious Agendas

There are numerous factors that can determine the nature of the hospital chaplain functions. Most of these factors have to do with the expectations of the hospital, denomination, and training. As a hospital chaplain, you may find yourself challenged to suppress or compromise some of your *religious* convictions relative to prayer, Scripture reading, evangelism, and theological orientation. These may become religious agendas that you intentionally or unintentional impose upon patients. Such aggressive conduct is always inappropriate for a chaplain.

Prayer and Scripture Agendas

Many chaplains consider Scripture reading and prayer an important and necessary function of pastoral care. However, *prayer and Scripture* reading must not be used inappropriately (see Appendix 2). They must not be forced upon people. When forced on patients, knowing and understanding the patient is no longer the primary concern. Hospital chaplains must never seek to force Scripture or prayer upon a patient.

Evangelism

Some chaplains may feel it's their duty to make sure patients accept Jesus Christ as their personal savior, especially if the patient is near death. A chaplain's work is not the work of an evangelist. Although it is the will of God that none should perish (2 Peter 3:9), it is equally clear that no person can come to the Father unless he/she is drawn by God (John 6:44). When a patient is drawn by God's Spirit, he/she will ask, "What must I do to be saved?"

Training Orientation

Clinical Pastoral Education (CPE) can be of great value for a chaplain and is mandatory for becoming a certified chaplain. These four Units (1600 hours) of extensive and intensive training help prepare a pastor to become a competent chaplain. However, CPE can be a problem when the chaplain begins to play the role of junior psychologist. The trainee needs to keep his/her eyes focused on the true role of the chaplain: To represent God. Where does a hospital chaplain find a perfect example for his/her role model? The answer is clearly found in the person of Jesus Christ. Jesus Christ is the perfect minister of pastoral care. Being the divine Son of God, His ministry was always without prejudice, totally characterized by the manifestation of love and presence of God. Although He did not minister in a hospital, He did minister to sick, needy and hurting people. As a hospital chaplain, you must minister to the sick, needy, and hurting in His stead, and under His leading and power. Full consideration must be given your preparation to visit. You must prepare yourself by viewing visitation as God's work and doing all you can to follow His lead (Proverbs 3:5-6) and by becoming familiar with and following institutional rules and polices.

To make your visits more effective and meaningful, you should collect, prepare, and properly use things such as Scripture verses, quotes, poems, and stories. Other things you can do to enhance your visitation ministry is to make your own handouts to help encourage patients, to make you own "Sorry I missed you" cards, and to make and maintain a resource and referral file.

In the area of personal development, the hospital chaplain must prepare himself/herself intellectually by gathering enough information to reduce the chances of being surprised. However, as a chaplain, you must be open to surprises such as rejection, horrible scenes, and false hopes or beliefs of those you visit. You must be prepared emotionally by realizing your own feelings, values, and beliefs. Mentally, you must be prepared by being conscious of your own weaknesses and strengths. You must be physically prepared by being aware of the way you dress and your personal hygiene. Maintaining a consistent and healthy relationship with God through daily devotions, prayer and Scripture reading will help you be prepared spiritually. Spiritual preparation is probably the essential ingredient that will make or break a hospital chaplain. You must have a heart for Jesus in order to have the heart of Jesus for others.

In the area of attitude, the hospital chaplain must keep in mind the importance of visitation and how it is on Jesus' list of things that please Him (See Matthew 25:31-35). God loves those of us who visit. According to James 1:27, pure and undefiled religion before the Father is to visit people in their afflictions and keep one's self unspotted from the world. Dear readers, people really need the help you can bring as a hospital chaplain.

In the area of personal skills, the hospital chaplain must be a good listener and show empathy. Listening is a form of servant-hood, a way to reach out and share the love of Christ. Listening can improve a person's life greatly. It allows people to get something off their minds. It establishes dialogue and helps you, as the chaplain, to respond properly. It provides an opportunity for empathy. Empathy is two people carrying the same burden. Empathy is an open heart that can do wonders. Listening and empathy allow you to be in tune with others' feelings. You must be dedicated to do the work of the kingdom. You must realize that everyone is not going to be healed (1 Peter 4:19). You may be a child of the Heavenly Father, but you must keep in mind that He makes the sun rise on both the evil and on the good, and sends rain on the just and on the unjust (Matthew 5:45).

Hospital chaplains cannot always plan the events that occur during a visit. However, it is good to develop a plan with the willingness to change your plan as the need dictates or the Holy Spirit leads. The worst things you can do is to presume upon a situation and then proceed with your own course of action (agenda). This is when you can miss the important things. This is why you don't find a lot of literature written about visitation. The clear design is to do your best and be flexible. Keep in mind that visiting experiences can be surprising. You can't always count on a specific plan of action. In your moment of shock, let God be your guide. You have to visit and learn. It's impossible to know about every visitation situation. You might have to go with the flow. Don't forget that it is God who prepares you and the patient for your visit.

Hospital chaplains must set goals to do their work. The main goal is to be the person God wants you to be. Goals are subject to change from blessing to survival. You might have an experience that will change you. The hospital chaplain's goal should never be given priority over God's leading presence. This makes your goal to be just what the Master wants you to be and to do according to the need at that moment (1 Thessalonians 4:3). Each goal will differ according to the spiritual needs of the person visited.

The hospital chaplain must approach a child who is a patient as a friend. Try to make them feel as comfortable as possible – smile and use a gentle voice. You must try to visit when the parent(s) is present. Don't get upset if the child is inattentive. Please keep in mind Matthew 19:14, which reminds us that, "for such is the kingdom of heaven."

The Hospital chaplain must approach a teen patient as a supporter. Teens usually don't have any idea how they are supposed to act. Don't expect any thanks for things like devotionals. Be patient with them. Don't lecture them or take advantage of situations where they have blundered. Prove that you care, rather than acting like you understand everything in the world.

The hospital chaplain must approach adult patients as a source of strength. Your goal is to carry as much of the adult's burden as possible. When proper, read a verse of Scripture, which may help them transfer their burden to God. Take their present condition into consideration. Listen to them and talk about things that interest them.

The hospital chaplain must approach elderly patients as a companion. Just being there can be a great achievement. Be careful about what you say to them. If they criticize the institution, don't join in. Do whatever you can to comfort them.

At all times, and especially during emergencies, hospital chaplains must wear their badge for identification. Carry a bible; you might need it. But avoid a large-sized Bible that might be intimidating to patients. Use your head (common sense) and God's wisdom. Don't be offensive. Talk loudly enough and in a natural tone. Don't draw attention to yourself; instead draw attention to God. Pray before you visit. Always talk to God about people before you talk to people about God. Ask them if they want you to pray. If so, then pray for their needs. Hug, touch, or hold hands when appropriate. Read Scripture slowly and with clarity. Avoid long passages of Scripture. Ask if they have a favorite Scripture.

The hospital chaplain ministry is special. It is what God wants for His people. As a chaplain, you must dress, talk, and act like God would act if He were in your shoes – because He is. Remember Paul's words: "For it is God which worketh in you both to will and to do his good pleasures" (Philippians 2:13).

The hospital chaplain needs to be sensitive to God-given opportunities to present the message of salvation (2 Timothy 4:2). Keep in mind that God prepares a person's heart before you come on the scene. You can take no credit for a person being saved. As it says in John 6:44, "No man come to me, except the Father which hath sent me draw him: and I will raise him up at the last day." As a chaplain, you can walk faithfully with God and be used of God to evangelize. By the way, evangelization is not proselytization. To proselytize is to coerce someone to believe what you believe. To evangelize is simply to share good news with people and to let them decide for themselves.

A hospital chaplain's ministry must be marked by joy, sincerity, and spiritual depth. Some people will be helped by simply being present with them, rather than from your words or your actions, but by being your God-filled self. Always maintain your faith.

Hospitals are full of patients complaining about not seeing anyone religious. There are many church folk who are complaining about not being visited. There is a difference between failed attempts to visit and pure negligence. It shouldn't take much motivation for you, as a hospital chaplain, to visit as many people as you can. You must not sit around waiting for a request. You must dedicate yourself to finding and helping those who really need you and your attentive and affirmative ministry of compassion.

Visiting can be fun if approached with the right attitude. It is not wise for unprepared people to visit. There are many possibilities of things you might encounter without warning. You might find a person in their last days, a person who is suicidal, grieving, lonely, addicted to drugs or alcohol, a sex offender, or many other possibilities that can make visiting tough. There are many people responses for you to deal with in a caring way. Some people are friendly and others may be unfriendly, hostile, defensive, or indifferent. It takes prayer and preparation to handle situations and responses encountered during visits. You never know what to expect. Don't let this scare you, just be prepared.

There is no reason for hospital chaplains to talk about theology. As a chaplain, you are not trying to get people to join anything. You are merely communicating God's concern over people's situations. To avoid discussing hot topics, you need to sometimes change the subject. Ask questions like, "What is your favorite bible verse? What is your favorite hymn?" Or talk about their care or family. There are many ways to deal with people without getting into deep theological discussions. Do everything you can to avoid arguments. You must not recommend or suggest any particular church.

It is a tough challenge for hospital chaplains to deal with non-talkers or hard-of-hearing patients. For these, you need to keep your visits short. Be pleasant and respectful. Read some verses, pray and then leave. Do not frustrate them. Accept the fact that they may not be able to communicate with you effectively. Don't take it personal. Don't be judgmental. Don't consider your visit a failure. It's a learning experience. And remember, you are still being supportive by simply being present with them.

When visiting disturbed or irrational behaving people, show them Jesus. Let your light shine before them. Give them an example of something that could be or could happen in their lives. Be yourself and be respectful. If you are enjoyable, nonjudgmental, and even human at times, you will do a lot to direct others toward a life that can be found only in Jesus the Christ. Be real and pure. Those who need to talk a lot let them talk – simply listen. As a hospital chaplain, you are going to encounter backsliders who may be reluctant to talk. This should not discourage you from helping to bring the backsliders to a full relationship with Jesus Christ. You must approach as one who would love to see the joy of life restored to a person. Try to get them to see that continuing in their negative path will be harmful to themselves and others.

When you encounter those patients who are disgruntled with the church and are mouthing off about it, advise the individual to talk to a person who is able to help the situation and bring about restoration. You should abort aggression by saying, "Let's stop right now and pray about this because what we are doing now isn't really helping the situation at all." God doesn't like division and you must avoid getting into the midst of divisive situations. If a person chooses to go this way, the chaplain must politely abstain. You can base your visitation ministry upon the assurance given in Romans 8:28, "And we can know that all things work together for good to them that love God, to them who are the called according to His purpose."

Hospital chaplains can use all the help they can get in the area of hospital ministry. This includes the things to do, the things not to do, what to watch for, contacts with the hospital and their expectations. There is a difference between the hospital chaplain who is there as an integral member of the healthcare team and others who merely come into the hospital for an occasional visit. There is protocol in a hospital. Acquaint yourself with hospital visitation times and policies. Upon entering the hospital check in at the information desk. Remember that although you might be a pastor, you are still a visitor. Approach properly and not arrogantly. Show that you care on your first visit. Most hospital stays are for only two days or less. Early discharges are likely and can change things. Let the Holy Spirit guide you. Keep in mind that healthcare workers, other professionals, family and church workers are usually involved in meeting all kinds of needs. This means you may be doing a lot of coordinating. Don't be a one-man show. You have to work with others in providing spiritual care to patients. It's a team effort. Don't be a know it all. Remember the important one is the patient. Minister in humility. The patient is in need of real love and care.

Enter the hospital as part of a healing team. Accept and be willing to work with all chaplains regardless of gender. First John 4:9 says, "In this was manifested the love of God toward us, because that God sent His only begotten Son into the world, that we might live through Him." All chaplains live through Him. Hopefully, each member of the team is listening to God as to what his/her role is. The hospital team considers themselves to be a part of an effective network, working on behalf of the patients. In the hospital, it is a necessity to work closely with others. Go with the flow. The more conscientious you present yourself the more cooperation you will enjoy. Knock before entering a room. Wash your hands before and after each visit. Avoid kissing and touching inappropriately. The best behavior is as little body contact as possible. Politely excuse yourself when a doctor or nurse comes to see your patient. Be mindful of your perfume or deodorant. Know yourself and what you can withstand. Show good bedside manners. Don't interrupt patients' and caretaker's conversations. Pray and let God guide you. James says, if you lack wisdom ask God (James 1:5). Don't adjust or sit on patient's bed. Always consider patients' limitations and conditions. Be honest – don't lie to patients. Be aware of distractions, other patients, and length of your visit. Be sensitive. Be sincere. Ask good questions. Don't pry. Let them talk because talking can be therapeutic. Let verses of Scripture you use grow out of the conversation. Minister to the blind and physically challenged as you minister to others. Bring comfort and hope to them. Help them deal with their emotional and spiritual distress. Let them know you feel privileged to be there. Be a good listener and speak encouraging words.

Be willing to serve patients communion. Combine this act of remembering Christ with Scripture and prayer. Make sure you check with the nurse to see if they can consume the elements, which represent our Lord's body and blood.

Prayer is important, never leave without prayer – unless the patient doesn't want you to pray. Talk to God for others. Seek God's strength and intervention on behalf of others. Praying for another brings them to God in your spirit. Prayer is seeking to bring someone to the throne of God who doesn't have the power, ability or belief to pray for himself/herself. God will be our strength when we are weak. He has made it so we can exchange our weakness, fears, and other emotions for His strength (Isaiah 40: 29-31). God will raise us above our troubling situations so we can bear them.

When ministering in the emergency room, the hospital chaplain must immediately seek God's intervention and pray. Do not offer a lot of explanation or read a lot of Scripture. Listen attentively and hear things people don't say. Let them talk. Carry your bible. Be calm. Don't allow other's attitudes or behaviors to discourage you. Be there. Be everything they need. Bring the love of Christ. Allow them to see Christ in you. Help them accept the loss as a part of life. Help them bring closure to their grief. Don't be afraid to ask questions. Don't be in a hurry to leave. Don't panic. Act as if an emergency is not a big deal. Be patient. Console family members when they feel mistreated. Be a peacemaker. Say a short, meaningful prayer or hug them. Bring a confident and compassionate face. Let them know who you are. Speak encouraging words. Treat all surgery as critical. Be prepared for rejection. Come early and stay late, if necessary. Stay with the family.

When visiting the ICU, identify yourself. Don't be discouraged if the patient is non-responsive. Be open to their request. Be sensitive. Don't ask a lot of questions. Imagine what they feel. Don't be distracted by all the sights and smells. Pray silently. Minister to them. Many of the ICU patients may be comatose. When visiting comatose patients, visit by faith. Represent the Master. Act as if the patient can hear you. ICU time is hope time. Remember God is there to help you. Inspire faith and faith in God's faithfulness (Lamentations 3:25). Empower them to wait on the Lord.

Visiting a contagious person can be dangerous to your own health. Observe all warning signs. If in doubt, ask questions. Be as brief as possible. Don't touch the patient or his/her bed or anything else in the room unless you have put on proper protective clothing (gloves, gown and mask). Wash your hands and face as soon as possible after the visit. When visiting AIDS patients, don't touch any blood or open wounds. But remember, AIDS patients are not contagious. So stand close and care for them.

When visiting the recovery room, recognize that this room is highly restricted. There may not be a need for you to visit here. However, sometimes as the hospital chaplain you may visit for the sake of giving a report to the patient's family.

Burn units are tough places for any one to visit. It's a place of desperation, pain and discomfort. Don't try to answer their why questions (See Psalm 73:1-26). As you enter, go to the desk and ask what to wear and how long to stay. Bring joy and a message of hope. Let them know you are privileged to be there. Listen to them. Speak encouraging words to them. Read to them. Some appropriate Scriptures to read are Psalm 100 and Psalm 73. Sing to them. Say a meaningful prayer, focusing on the person for whom you want God to intervene.

Nursing homes are full of some of the loneliest people in the world. Many are in varying stages of depression and grief. They are sometimes embarrassed because they can't help themselves. They often think they are a burden to their families. Give yourself to them. Share the love God has for them. Show them that you really care for them. Be nonjudgmental. Read them stories. Let them talk about their families and show them empathy. Help them if they feel rejected by their own families. Be truthful and honest with them. If appropriate, serve them communion. Provide music and prayer. Bring young people and pets around them. Arrange a revisit.

Alzheimer's patients lose their memory. It tears them up because they want to grab their memory but can't. They become like children again. They do understand a lot, so you will be able to minister to them. Do not test their memory. Minister to them as a stranger – with love, concern, and openness to the needs they share. Do not place any requirements upon them. Act as if nothing is wrong. Make it easy on them (Psalm 73:26). Bring joy and sincerity with you. Let them know you feel privileged to be there. Bring flowers, cards or other appropriate things with you. Listen to them. Speak encouraging words to them. Read as much as they can handle. Pray a meaningful prayer for them. Ask if you can revisit.

Ministering to the terminally ill can be one of the most important and meaningful visits you can make. You will wish you could do something to take away the pain and misery. Realize you are helpless and all you can bring is love, empathy and the desire to be a caregiver (1 Corinthians 13:4). It is important for you to know the stages of grief in response to terminal illness. However, don't attempt to use this knowledge to diagnose your patients. Keep in mind that grief is not the same for all people. The first stage of grief is shock and confusion. Some find knowledge of their condition overwhelming. They don't know whether to cry or get a second opinion or take off to the woods never to be heard of again. The question "Why?" arises. Patiently stand by their side. No words are necessary. They may just need a shoulder to cry on. Don't go into denial yourself and say something dumb like, "This can't happen. God wouldn't allow this." This is a good time to maybe read Psalm 139:1-18. The second stage of grief is denial. Some may become so overwhelmed that they might be retreating by denying that it's even happening. They might say, "This can't be happening to me. It's just a dream or something. I will go to sleep and when I wake up it will all be over." There are no words; they don't know what to believe. If possible, reason with them. The third stage of grief is anger. After accepting the fact of what is happening, they feel this is not fair. They were good Christians. God isn't fair. They might withdraw and become nasty. They might be angry with those who will go on living after they die. They might be mad because they think that they are the only one going through this. Share with them the fact that their anger is a normal reaction. Also share that this anger may not only be hurting them, but it might cause those who want to help to withdraw from them. The fourth stage of grief is bargaining. Some attempt to make a deal with God. For example: "God if you spare me, I will serve you for the rest of my life." Just go along with them. They will soon work through this and discover that their future is in God's hand. Keep your counsel soft. The fifth stage of grief is depression. Depression is a deep emotional condition that is easy to get stuck in, especially if the patient has suffered loss and has nothing much to look forward to.

Depressed patients feel hopeless or in despair. Let them know that the Lord has been to the depth of depression (See Matthew 26:38). Don't let them go through it alone. Don't try to explain it. Come alongside like the Holy Spirit does for you. Be sure you have a support group for yourself or you may be in depression too. The sixth and final stage of grief is yielding. Jesus is our example (See Luke 22:42). From this point on your visits will become easier. Be patient if they backslide or get stuck in other stages. Whatever happens, be there (See Hebrews 6:10). Allow them to have their feelings without judging them. Feelings are not right or wrong. Terminally ill patients have different feelings. They might not feel helpless. Use your imagination. Try to understand what the person feels when everything in his/her survival seems out of his/her hands. They may depend on others for brief times of joy. They might feel fearful. Fear of the unknown is the greatest of all fears. The fear of death is common. The journey to death is challenging. Yet it's a journey we must all take. You can help where they are through your compassionate listening, understanding words and sincere dedication. It's okay for a Christian to have fear – just don't let it replace the faith needed to finish life's journey with joy, confidence, and hope (Psalm 23:4). If appropriate, share John 11:25-26. Then ask, "Do you believe this?" They might feel hopeless. It's a terrible thing to feel hopeless. Encourage them without giving them a false hope. There is always hope. All things are possible with God. They might feel lonely and abandoned. They are alone; the world they are leaving is going on. They will make everyone they love feel bad for a long time. They feel abandoned because no one can go with them. Every visit to the terminally ill is an opportunity to make a person's last days, days of less grief and more days of loving care. Help the caregivers and family members in any way you can. Research the patient's diseases and conditions to help you better understand and respond to their physical ordeal.

As a hospital chaplain, the hardest thing you will have to do is tell a person he/she is dying. Be sure you are spiritually and mentally prepared within yourself. If you are struggling with the reality of your own death, it will be more difficult for you to make it easier for others. If you are to help others, you must believe John 11:25-26. Once you become filled with God and not the fear of death, you will be prepared to help others. Tell them sympathetically, but plainly, that their loved one has died. Assure them that death is part of life. Comfort them.

Hospital chaplains must be careful with recommendations. You should be cautious about giving your opinions. Whether it is about placing someone in a nursing home or the use of life support and heroic measures, these are matters for families to decide. Your main focus should be on helping the patient and family prepare for death. Encourage them to make wills or living wills and make plans for handling issues related to funeral services, belongings, bills, insurances, property, etc.

In the process of death, a person might feel alone and isolated. No one really knows exactly what he/she feels. They may lose interest in things they like. They might become tired and sleep a lot. They may lose their appetite. This can be a sign that they are nearing the end. Make sure they are comfortable. They may drift in and out of reality. Any movement may take a lot of strength. They might become confused. Bodily functions, blood pressure, body temperature and breathing can change with impending death. Days or hours before they leave this earth, behavior and body signs may become irregular. This is when you want to stay close, hold their hand, read your Bible, and sing songs even more than you have before. Make the scene lovely. Remember this is no time for heavy discussions. Restlessness may increase along with lung and throat congestion. Make sure their lips are kept moist and heart happy. Breathing may stop for a while. Their eyes may stay open as they stare, and they might not recognize you. Their body color may change and they might begin to get colder. At times they may take shallow breaths and then there will be no more. The body finally shuts down. At that moment they go into the presence of God (2 Corinthians 5:8). They leave the shell they lived in here on earth.

Grief recovery is a process of remembering with less pain. Grief recovery varies from person to person. People must be allowed to recover at one's own pace. There are stages of recovery. The first stage of recovery is to let go and let God. God is the first and greatest source of strength and healing. You must help the grieving person begin recovery by allowing God into their deepest pain. As a hospital chaplain, you must always try to invite God into the healing process, realizing that He totally understands and will help. The second stage of recovery is for the grieving person to learn what grief is. You must help them understand that grief is a shock absorber and very natural. Grief is an emotional response to loss. The third stage of recovery is to accept the reality and experience of pain. It will help them adapt to their situation when you lead them to believe and accept that their loss is real. The fourth stage of recovery is saying a final goodbye. It is a difficult thing to do, but life goes on. You must convince the grieving person to go on with their life and make it enjoyable.

Death is not our final enemy. It's a part of life and God will be with us when we place our life in His care. Keep trusting. Never stop believing. And always have faith.

As a hospital chaplain, you should keep a journal and be consistently aware of your performance in pastoral care. You must keep a record of your visits. I keep a record of patients visited and the results of each visit. A copy of the form I use can be found in the Appendix 1 (Hospital Chaplain's Visitation Form).

CHAPTER 3

Hospital Chaplain and Differences

———⟫●⟪———

Differences are those distinguishing characteristics that let us know that all human beings are not alike. As a hospital chaplain, you will have to respect the differences others bring in order to minister effectively to them. You must respect others' culture, worldviews, and religions.

Some healthcare workers, including hospital chaplains, may be unfamiliar with multi-cultural needs and requirements in dealing with patients. In our country, where cultures are intermingled, the practices of a particular culture, which includes its religious aspects, must be dealt with in a respectful and productive manner. Healthcare workers have the reputation of being caring and understanding people. Because of this, they do not make light of people's beliefs and customs. In most hospitals, when patients are admitted, they are presented with a form that requests information about their religion, diet, etc. Christian pastoral care in the hospital is carried out in the name of Jesus Christ across cultural and religious lines. As a chaplain, you will provide spiritual care for all. You will respect a person's right to have his/her own religious beliefs. You will not use manipulation or pressure to affect a change in a person's religious beliefs or practices.

Culture can be defined as intellectual and artistic achievement or expression. Culture in its true form is an integration of reasoning, knowledge, thinking, and that which is natural. The United States has become what many call a multi-cultural society. Due to the fact that illness and sickness has no respect of culture, people of these different cultures will be treated in hospitals throughout the nation. This means that as a hospital chaplain, you will be challenged to minister to patients with varying levels of reasoning, knowledge, thinking, and that which is natural to them, but not to you.

It is impossible for you to become fully knowledgeable of every culture, but it is important that you know something about the major or more influential cultures in the United States. Culture influences some religions and religion influences some cultures. Either way, what people believe and practice is related to their culture. You must keep in mind that when people become hospitalized they don't part with their culture. To be effective in offering and providing spiritual support to all patients, you must take into consideration a patient's culture. You must try to figure out the patient's level of reasoning, knowledge, thinking, and what he/she considers to be normal.

As a hospital chaplain, you must be able to minister to patients having contrasting or competing views of life and the world. You will use your own worldview as the standard in which to make a comparison. All views must be looked at as coping mechanisms. Coping mechanisms that give a person a set of basic outlooks that help explain the pattern of good and bad things, good and bad people, pain and pleasure, spiritual uplifting experiences versus spiritually depressing ones, and much more.

As a hospital chaplain, you must be aware of the influences and pressures a multi-cultural society will have upon your Christian faith. You must not allow your Christian view to be erased, while in a trance-like state of acceptance, believing nothing is wrong with false or less than rational beliefs or practices. You must allow Jesus to guard your heart and mind until the day of the Lord. Remember, you know God. He is the Creator of the heavens and the earth. He is eternal and everlasting. He is not bound by time or temporal elements as humans are. He is over and above time. He exists at all times and can be located at all times. He is a Spirit. He is the maker and source of all that is. He can intervene at any time and under any condition to make things happen. He is almighty God.

It is important for you note that God is not part of the world. He is independent of the world. He transcends the world. He puts His Holy Spirit within hospital chaplains to cause them to act out and to will according to His good purpose. Do all things to His glory. Bless the Lord through your life and ministry.

Plato believed that everything that is alive or exists in our world of time and change was created through the knowledge of heavenly forces. Plato was off because of his eternizing. You must always be reminded of the nature of God and the words of Jesus:

> *Lay not for yourselves treasures on earth, where moth and rust doth corrupt and where thieves break through and steal. But lay up for yourselves treasures in heaven, where neither moth nor rust doth corrupt, and where thieves do not break through nor steal. For where your treasure is,* there will *your heart be also.* (Matthew 6:19-21)

In Christ we find the real hope that no other worldview or belief system can give. Other world religions portray God as mischievous, unpredictable, or impersonal. God in the Christian tradition is altogether completely free as a person to act. He is only constrained by his own nature. He is from Himself. He explains His own existence. He exists because of His nature. It is in His nature to exist. He is an independent being. He is the eternal source of the universe (Acts 17:24-28).

Your conception of God should be that He is perfect in knowledge, power, being, and everything else. As the second person of the Godhead, He took on flesh and dwelt among men, was crucified, buried, rose on the third day, spent 40 more days ministering on earth, then ascended up into heaven where He waits for His enemies to be made His footstool and for His return. Some world religions, apart from Christianity, will picture God as being perfect, yet too transcendent for us to be in a relationship with Him. Or He will be too manlike, animal-like or creation-like, so we can relate to

Him and know this God, but He will not be perfect. He will not have the power to independently exist or to raise Himself from the dead, etc.

Many atheists say there is a problem with evil. Christianity makes a necessary case for evil. According to Scripture, man by nature has become wicked, apart from God, lost (Ephesians 2). Some worldviews reject the idea that man is radically evil and accept the idea that man is basically good. As a Christian, you must maintain that man is wicked by nature. However, to impose this belief on a patient would be inappropriate

You must hold on to your faith with the understanding that other people will hold on to their beliefs out of total commitment and will not give up their belief unless affected by the compelling and changing power of the Holy Spirit. You will find that some are more objective with respect to learning and changing their presuppositions. You must always be mindful of the role the Holy Spirit plays in convicting the heart and converting a person from one worldview to the worldview of Christianity. The Christian's belief-forming mechanisms are from the hand of the one and true God.

Crucial experiment is whereby you can either verify or falsify a hypothesis or theory. Every worldview probably has a crucial experiment or pivotal belief. If that pivotal belief can be proven true, the worldview will be true. If the pivotal belief can be proven false, then the worldview will be false. The crucial experiment for Christianity is the resurrection from the dead of Jesus Christ. In 1 Corinthians 15:14-20 we find these words:

> *And if Christ be not risen, then is our preaching vain, and your faith is also vain. Yea, and we are found false witnesses of God; because we have testified of God that he rose up Christ: whom he raised not up, if so be that the dead raise not. For if the dead rise not, then is not Christ raised: And if Christ be not raised, your faith is vain; ye are yet in your sins. Then they also which are fallen asleep in Christ are perished. If in this life only we have hope in Christ, we are of all men most miserable. But*

now is Christ risen from the dead, and become first
fruits of them that slept.

It is not clear what the crucial experiment in Islam or Buddhism would be. The crucial experiment for secular humanism would be evolutionary theory. All worldviews will seemingly have counter examples. However, if God exists, and He does, then regardless of what view people may adopt, God is still going to afford everyone an opportunity to be saved. Wisdom alone tells us, regardless of our presuppositions or selected views that we still are responsible as humans to do and not do certain things. Simply treat people the way they want to be treated. Respect their culture, their views and religions.

The following are a few examples of how you, as a hospital chaplain, can properly minister to patients with varying differences or opposing views.

The patient is from Israel and his/her religion is Judaism. How do you best provide spiritual and emotional support for the Jewish patient? If possible, you should contact a Rabbi. In the case of impending death and unavailability of a Rabbi or fellow Jew, you may read Psalm 23, 103, and/or 139 aloud. Your last words should be, "Hear O Israel, the Lord our God, the Lord is one."

The patient is from India and of the Hindu faith. How do you best provide spiritual and emotional support for the Hindu patient? If possible you should call in a Hindu priest. The Hindu priest will help in all spiritual matters. Keep in mind that accepting death philosophically is a trait of Hinduism. The priest, when available, fulfills the role of facilitating acceptance. A devout Hindu may desire to read the Hindu Scriptures, particularly the *Bhagavad Gita*. It may be a good idea for you to have a copy of the Hindu Scriptures available.

The patient is from Iraq and his/her religion is Islam. How do you best provide spiritual and emotional support for the Muslim patient? When possible, you should contact an Iman (religious leader) to hear confession of sins. If there is no Iman, it must be left to the family to read from the Koran. In the case of impending death, the family washes and prepares the body for death. If no relatives are available, then any Muslim can be asked to help.

The patient is a United States born citizen and his/her religion is Christianity. How do you best provide spiritual and emotional support for the Christian patient? First, learn the denomination of the patient. Then attempt to connect them to their belief affiliation. Denomination affiliation or non-affiliation often determines the type of practices and beliefs the patient may subscribe to. You must remember that spiritual and emotional support is always carried out in the name of Jesus the Christ. This could involve reading Scripture, praying, administering communion, counseling or helping in some other way with the patients' or families' permission.

There are many more differences or opposing views to Christianity. There are cultures within cultures in our mixed up world. The challenges these cultures impose upon the hospital chaplain are great. You must study to show yourself approved to minister in the multi-cultural hospital environment. You must respect the patient's culture, opposing views and beliefs, while at the same time realizing that what you have to offer is of a divine nature and culture. I personally view Christianity as being a heavenly culture.

CHAPTER 4

The Hospital Chaplain and Crisis Counseling

—————>⊶<—————

The hospital chaplain's role as counselor is to discover the nature of the patient's spiritual and emotional needs at that moment and to meet those needs, whatever they may be. For the hospital chaplain, this can be considered crisis counseling. This is providing immediate intervention to reach and instant resolution to prevent a lost opportunity. A crisis is a short-term experience that can impose danger and opportunity at the same time.

There is uniqueness to crisis counseling. That uniqueness is because of the brevity of a crisis and the kind of counseling that needs to be done. Counseling for people in crisis situations is more directive and dramatic than counseling for those with long-term issues of life. A good hospital chaplain learns to deal with his/her own problems and out of that helps others to deal with their problems.

A crisis is not a reason to fear or panic. It's a time of great opportunity to help others with their problems. A crisis never conveniently occurs on one's schedule. They just happen spontaneously. You have to be prepared for a crisis to occur at any potential point and inconvenient time. People are usually more receptive during a crisis situation and may welcome the short-term counseling you have to offer.

Hospital chaplains, in approaching a crisis situation, must consider the lack of time and deal with the problem immediately. You must keep in mind you're not to build long-term relationships, but be committed to immediate action and results. You will want to use the Word of God to deal with the needs of individuals, as they can be brought to immediate change and therefore, immediate hope.

Effective questioning is a part of good counseling. You are not only there to listen, but to also ask the kind of questions that will give directions to patients and their families according to the facts. As you ask questions, you will begin to understand what happened and how the situation got started and out of hand, and their perception of the situation. Intervention involves challenge, support, evaluation, feedback, recommendation, and agreement. Keep in mind that there must be an end to the counseling process. Termination is important because it says to the person, "You don't need me any more. You can now handle the problem on your own. God is there to help you meet your need."

Responses to a crisis vary, depending upon the individual. Some people respond with depression, others with heightened anxiety, and some go into shock. Others respond in violence and some in false adaptation. False adaptation is a problem for Christians. Some Christians are prone to suppress anger, worry, fear, and other feelings, and go on like everything is just fine.

The following skills are needed in order to provide adequate counseling in a crisis situation: a realistic perspective of the problem, a holistic orientation, an understanding of the essentials of flexibility and a balance between empathy and strength. During interaction, you have to counsel for the duration of the crisis and understand the severity of the trauma and pre-trauma personality of the patient.

The pitfalls hospital chaplains must be aware of are: (1) Taking over a person's life. (2) Giving a false assurance. (3) Focusing on the solution not the cause. (4) Assuming the meaning of the trauma. (5) Failing to remain calm. (6) Over estimating or under estimating the situation. (7) Failing to ask for help. (8) Assuming all crises is alike.

There are basic approaches to crisis problems. The problem solving approach is suggested with its goal of confronting the problem and bringing it to a solution. There are three normal steps of action to be taken in crisis intervention. They are assessment, planning, and intervention. Assessment leads to planning and planning to intervention.

What it boils down to is how a person handles the pressure. If the balancing factors are present in their life, then the end result will be a realistic view of the pressure, needed situational support, good coping mechanisms, personal responsibility, and prevention of a crisis. They will be able to face the normal stresses and strains of life. If the balancing factors are not present, then the opposite result can be expected.

The wrong view of situations causes a person to get bitter instead of resolving their problem. When a distorted view takes over, there will be no situational support or coping mechanism. Coping mechanisms are both internal and external. Situational support has to do with friends, neighbors, relatives, and family members who help people through their crisis.

The crisis may affect individuals differently. People may view the same situation differently. Different people give different input into a crisis. In the area of coping, remember you are not only trying to help the person survive the crisis, but also help the person decide what to do in the middle of the crisis.

There are two basic types of crises. A situational crisis caused by a situation that brings about stress in a person's life, and maturity stages of a person's life that lead to a crisis of adjustment or development, such as adolescence, adulthood, mid-life crisis, old age, etc.

Physical illness has a diversified affect on people as any other problem they can face in life. When some people are told they are ill, they may go immediately home and act sick. Others may deny that they are sick. They don't believe anything could be wrong with them that could limit them at all or threaten their employment situation. They will use every mechanism of denial in dealing with the problem of physical illness. Physical illness may be the best thing in the world for a Christian. It may cause him/her to look at life more honestly than he/she would under normal circumstances. It may provide an opportunity for him/her to strengthen their relationship with God and family.

Suicide is not as much of a crisis as it is the end of a crisis. It is the end result of a stressful situation in which a person goes through a series of feelings. Some of the causes of suicide are loss of worthiness, a sense of hopelessness, loss of meaning, loss of purpose and lack of direction. As a chaplain, you must take serious all threats of suicide. Suicide intervention counseling is a very complex process. It may involve a number of factors. You may need to refer an individual to a psychiatrist. The patient may need to remain hospitalized or be detained for his or her own protection. This is the area of intervention where the team affect is desperately important and necessary.

Life is filled with problems. They are a natural part of our daily experiences and part of our life long journey here on earth. Learning to handle the problems of life is one step of spiritual maturity in life. The Bible, in 2 Corinthians 1:3-7, tells us that God allows us to go through troubles so we can comfort others during their troubles. The more you suffer the more you will be able to understand the problems, needs, and suffering of others. God chooses to use problems to make us better people. Everybody has problems. Every problem is a temporary situation.

Every problem has a limitation and time span. Every problem in life will change you one way or another. They will make you bitter or better. Try to develop a personal perspective on problems. Ask yourself, "What is it that God wants me to do with this problem?" If you want people to handle their problems properly, then help them face reality, take responsibility and do right as opposed to doing wrong. Remember that right is taught and defined in your Bible.

You must breakdown communication barriers to be an effective counselor. Through communications we are either building barriers or bridging gaps (reaching out and over barriers with communication). Communication breakdown drives people away from God and from one another. God created human beings with the ability to communicate with Him and one another.

For many people death is the greatest problem of life. Many people don't like to talk about it or attend funerals. We are afraid to deal with death. Trying to hold on to life creates a fear of death or to have phobia about death. Many of us fear death instead of fearing

God, who is the source of life. For the Christian, death means eternal life. As the hospital chaplain, you must point people to an eternity beyond their immediate experience in this world (2 Corinthians 5:8; Daniel 12:2).

Learning to deal with failure, helping people face and handle failure properly, and building success in their lives, is one of the most important aspects of counseling. The biblical definition of failure is to give up. It is the opposite of success. Sin is a form of failure (Roman 3:23). Everyone fails and has limitations, but everyone also has abilities. Failure is a normal part of life. If we are going to help others deal with failure, then we must have an understanding of success. Genuine success is doing the will of God as revealed in His Word. Failure is not the end of life. It does not end your relationship with God because of His extended grace.

Human suffering, whether it's physical, emotional or spiritual, is one of the major problems of life. Suffering is part of a reality of life. It's one of the major crises that hospital chaplains have to deal with. Suffering is a deep inner stress. According to the Bible, God is the one who comforts us in all troubles (2 Corinthians 1:3-7). Suffering is part of His purpose and plan in our lives, to shape us in the image of Christ and bring glory to Himself. Suffering is character revealing and character building. Suffering has meaning and purpose (Romans 8:28). As a hospital chaplain, you must always be mindful that it is God who gives meaning, purpose and direction in life.

CHAPTER 5

The Hospital Chaplain and Comforting

———————

For the hospital chaplain, the word *comfort* means to impart strength and hope. As a chaplain, your comforting will include the idea of soothing distress or depression. In the act of bringing comfort you are one who stands beside a person to give encouragement when he/she is undergoing severe pressure. You are there to be with them, to bring hope, and to encourage them in their time of need.

Life's journey for human beings is incomplete without suffering (1 Corinthians 1:5). This incompleteness in the life of others provides you, as a hospital chaplain, with opportunities to comfort others with the comfort you have received from God (2 Corinthians 1:3,4). You will find many Christians and non-Christians in situations, even seemingly unbearable conditions, in which they can use some comfort. As the hospital chaplain, you must learn about these situations and make yourself available to these people. Now I am going to share with you four situations in which we are called upon to bring comfort.

Family Grief
We must do all we can to comfort family members experiencing grief. Sometimes it's difficult to stand by quietly and watch family

members experiencing grief following the death of a loved one. You might feel that unless you are doing something you are not being helpful at all. At this time, it might be helpful for you to think of yourself as a friend. If appropriate, reach out and put your arm around a family member's shoulder or hold their hand. But look for their reaction to your touching. Some people don't like to be touched. If you feel like crying with them, go ahead; however, exercise self-control. Remember you have responsibilities to God and the family. Just being there may be the most helpful thing you can do. Religious beliefs help many people cope with death. Their faith in God is a strong support mechanism. Always note the family's denominational association. Respect their beliefs even if they differ from your own. You must understand that many religions/denominations practice different rites. They may have different customs and beliefs relative to death. When possible, accompany the family in viewing the body. Seeing the body may help them accept the death as a reality. Stay with them throughout the grieving process. Make sure they are provided proper counseling. Help them cope with their grief. Say kind words. Read appropriate Scripture verses. Show love and pray when proper. Always be considerate and flexible.

The Confused

We all have experienced some degree of confusion in our lives. Without a doubt most of us have encountered confused or disoriented persons. We need to know how to bring comfort to these people. We must become familiar with some of the causes of confusion. Being in a strange environment may, in some cases, be the cause of confusion. Confusion may also stem from alcohol withdrawal, acute infection, head trauma, drug usage, and other physical conditions. You can usually identify confusion in a person by investigating puzzling or bizarre behavior (such as when a person calls you someone else). Never assume that bizarre behavior accompanies all confusion. A person may appear content and quiet, but still be completely disoriented. Always suspect confusion or impending confusion when the person becomes increasingly restless and apprehensive, doesn't respond to your questions or has difficulty concentrating, acts bewildered, shows fluctuations in mood, actions and rationality, acts jumpy and irritable when disturbed, seems preoccupied most of the time, and has frequent crying or laughing spells.

Don't assume confusion without thoroughly investigating each sign and symptom. Spend as much time as possible with them, if they respond positively to your presence. Speak softly. Refuse to argue. Speak in one-thought sentences. Give them the spiritual and emotional support they need. Help them connect with reality. No matter how senseless they sound, don't assume what they are saying has no connection to reality. Be concerned. Show love. Be sincere. Ask God to help you.

The Depressed

First, you must know what causes a person to become depressed. Most people become depressed because they feel they have suffered some real or imagined loss. For example, loss of health, body image, job, loved ones, etc. You can expect temporary depression in people who are grieving. Don't spend time trying to analyze the person's problems. Do what you can to offer spiritual and emotional help, while you continue to assess his/her condition. If his/her condition seems severe or prolonged, take measures to refer the person immediately for psychiatric help. Be aware that certain medications can also cause depression in patients. The patient's doctor can treat that problem.

Second, once you are familiar with the causes, learn to recognize the physical and emotional signs of depression. Watch for erratic sleep patterns, apathy, appetite loss, complaints of headaches, fatigue, reduced sex drive, profound sadness with crying spells, hostility towards others and self, and anxiety or despair with strongly expressed fears of death.

You can bring comfort by accepting the person as they are. Don't reject them by saying things like, "What's the matter with you?" "Things aren't that bad," or "You're not acting like a Christian." Such remarks suggest they have no right to feel depressed. Don't be judgmental. Instead ask, "Why do you feel that way?" Discuss his/her feelings. Reinforce positive behavior. Be friendly. Show love. When possible, share Scripture and pray. Seek God's help.

The Terminally Ill or Dying

It's a known fact that no two people react to dying or death in the exact same manner. We, as a society, want to believe and accept the idea that dying people go through certain stages in the process of dying. This helps us anticipate and meet the dying person's needs. However, we must realize that many dying people will not follow a step-by-step pattern. Even so, there are similarities in many respects.

Dr. Elisabeth Kubler-Ross gives us the five stages of grief of a person who has been told that he/she has a fatal illness (See *On Death and Dying*, MacMillan, 1967). Dr. Kubler-Ross' five steps of grief are shock and denial, anger, bargaining, depression, and acceptance. During the shock and denial stage, they refuse to believe that the diagnosis was correct. During the anger, bargaining and depression stages, they progress from, "No not me!" to "Yes me, but..." to simply, "Yes." In the acceptance stage they say, "I am ready to go." The person is not happy, but not terribly sad either. Keep in mind Hebrews 9:27, which reminds us that after death comes judgment.

To help a person move through the process of dying to a peaceful death, you must work to relieve loneliness, depression, and fears. Be there for them. Encourage and help their relatives and friends to be supportive. Help them prepare for their death. Remember that a person who is prepared to die is prepared to live. Be patient. Avoid clichés such as, "Everything is going to work out fine," or "You're looking well," or "You'll be up and about in no time." He/she knows they probably won't be up and about again. And a patient certainly knows how he/she looks. Don't be fraudulent. Don't give false hope. Give them honest answers. Try hard to understand what he/she is experiencing. Watch how you carry yourself in their presence. Help them accept dying as being as much a part of life as birth. Comfort them. Leave them with all the comfort you can offer. Pray before you speak with them. Share some comforting words with them. Follow God's lead. Respect their decision and be concerned about their final need. Remember bringing one into the kingdom of God is God's work. You are there to walk them home with love, compassion, and comfort. Remember

God is the source and supplier of your love, compassion, and comfort. He is the God of all comfort.

The Bible, in conjunction with life experiences, teaches us that suffering does not affect believers in Christ as it does non-believers. They react differently to suffering. The non-believers reaction is normally negative. In many cases, the reaction may be violent behavior. The believer's reaction is normally positive. In most cases the reaction is non-violent behavior. It is only in suffering that we can truly experience God's comforting presence – His mighty working power and victory in Jesus.

RESOURCES AND REFERENCES

Pugh, John. Course: *Theories of Personality*, Master's Divinity School, 1999, Newburgh, IN

Ammon, William H. Course: *The Chaplain In Action*, Master's Divinity School, 1999, Newburgh, IN

Eyrich, Howard A. & Vance, Russell E. Course: *Gerontology*, Master's Divinity School, 1999, Newburgh IN

Ammon, William H. Course: *A Biblical Approach to Death and Grief*, Master's Divinity School, 1999, Newburgh, IN

Hindson, Edward E. Course: *Crisis Counseling*, Master's Divinity School, 1999, Newburgh, IN

Martin, Edward. Course: *Christianity and Competing World Views*, Master's Divinity School, 1999, Newburgh, IN

H.C.M.A. Clinical Pastoral Training Curriculum, Hospital Chaplains' Ministry of America, Placentia, California

SUGGESTED READINGS

Eyer, Richard C. *Holy People, Holy Lives, Law and Gospel in Bioethics*, St. Louis, Missouri: Concordia Publishing House, 2000

Eyrich Howard A. & Dabler, Judy. *The Christian Handbook on Aging*, Keamey, Nebraska: Morris Publishing, 1990

Gerkin, Charles V. *An Introduction to Pastoral Care*, Nashville, Tennessee: Abingdon Press, 1997

Hindson, Ed, *Overcoming Life's Toughest Problems*, Eugene, Oregon: Harvest House Publishing, 1999

Kearon, Kenneth. *Medical Ethics: An Introduction*, Dublin, Ireland: The Columbia Press, 1999

Wright, H. Norman. *Crisis Counseling: What to Do During the First 72 Hours*, San Bernardino, California: Here's Life Publishers, Inc., 1991.

Mitchell, Jeffrey T. & Resnik, H.L.P. *Emergency Response To Crisis*, Ellicott City, Maryland: Chevron Publishing Corporation, 1986

Ammon, William. *Walking Our Loved One Home: Using Your Bible*, Kearny, Nebraska: Morris Publishing, 1995

APPENDIX 1

Chaplain's Visitation Record

Religion	Room Number & Bed	Name	Remarks (X = Prior Visit)

Asleep = sl
anxious = anx
brief witness = brief w
busy = busy MD/RN/Therapist, etc.
Jesus Christ = JC
Church = ch
Closed Door = dr cl
Company=(visitors) = co
Curtain pulled = curt pl
Depressed = dep
Speaks no English = no Eng
Expired = exp
Family = fam
God = G
Good Talk = GT
Good Visit = GV

Hard of Hearing = H of H
Holy Spirit = HS
Left Business Card = C
Much Talk = much T
No Church = no ch
No interest = NI
No pastor = no pas
Not Religious = not rel
Pastor = pas
Patient = PT
Prayer = pr
Prayer with witness = pr c w
Prayer before surgery = pr B4S
Problem = prob
Says Trusting = ST
Thank You = TY

Appropriate Scripture for Special Situations

Most, if not all, true Christians subscribe to the idea that no matter what our immediate need is, we can find help in Scripture, whenever we take time to look for it. Whatever we may sense, experience, want or expect, the Bible speaks to us about it. Here are some appropriate Scriptures hospital chaplains may use to minister to patients and their families.

Anger
Proverbs 16:32
Ecclesiastes 7:19
James 1:19,20 2

Comfort
Psalm 27:14
Psalm 46:1
Psalm 55:22
Matthew 11:28

Courage
Psalm 27:14
Psalm 31:24
Isaiah 40:29

Death
Psalm 23:4
Psalm 48:14
Psalm 49:15
John 3:15

Fear
Proverbs 41:13
Romans 8:15
Timothy 1:7
1 Peter 3:12-14

Hope
Psalm 31:24
Psalm 42:11
Psalm 71:5
1 Peter 1:3

Loneliness
Isaiah 58:9
John 14:18

Sickness
Exodus 23:25
Jeremiah 30:17
James 5: 14-16

CPSIA information can be obtained
at www.ICGtesting.com
Printed in the USA
BVHW07s1948250718
522612BV00011B/824/P